# writing

## the

# damn

# book

*How to start, write and publish a non-fiction book for creative people who have a hard time finishing things*

*Stacy Nelson*

# writing
## the
# damn
# book

*How to start, write and publish a non-fiction book for creative people who have a hard time finishing things*

BADASS PUBLISHING CO. | CALIFORNIA

Copyeditor: Donne Higton

Designer: Meg Sylvia - Artful Publications

ISBN-13: 978-0-9977501-0-2

BadAss Publishing Co. - Temecula, CA

www.BadAssPublishingCo.com

# READY TO
*Publish?*

Download your handy-dandy one page
Publishing Checklist at:

*wrtitingthedamnbook.com/checklist*

so you can not just Write the Damn
book, but Finish It as well!!!

*I am grateful* for my Inner & Outer Councils who push me into the ocean and expect me to swim, which I do...eventually. For kicking my backside until the damn book is published and for all the other books that they keep putting on my plate to write. Bring it on!

I'd like to send special love to my clients who have not only confirmed that this shit works, but who are my biggest mirrors in the world, inspiring the hell out of me daily.

I am sending deep gratitude for my Book Angels...who are responsible for getting me past those last few tedious details, and who fiercely support my work and are my Ambassadors in the world. Thank you for all you have done and will do.

And anyone else I haven't listed, I still love you. But this book belongs to them... XOXO

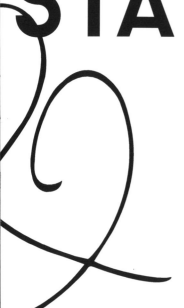

SECTION 01:

# STARTING

# GOOD TO
## *Great*

Going from a bad situation to a good situation makes sense to people. The bad is chasing you towards the good. There's purpose and reason to try, to struggle and to do things that will help you get from bad to good. The impetus is obvious – to get out of pain.

Going from good to great? Not quite as obvious or as urgent. Good is simply that – good. Why change that? Why shake up the status quo when you're good?

*If you're happy without great, there's nothing chasing you there urgently.*

So people dream of writing the book, but they are also good without it.

Writing a book takes effort and time and it's uncomfortable. It brings up fears and points out inadequa-

cies. It's a vulnerable process and it demands that you step up into your power and deliver something that is a statement of who you are in the world.

It's a step towards GREAT.

So it's easier to stay in the GOOD.

It's easier to dream about writing rather than get uncomfortable.

It's safer.

It's not urgent.

Growing from good to great takes more than just dreaming. It's when the want turns into a need…

So you read this book and stay 'good'. That's fine.

*But if you're willing to get uncomfortable and stretch, read the book and pause to take action between every step or contact me to have me alongside you for the journey at http://www.writingthedamnbook.com*

Going from Good to Great may not seem urgent, but I promise you that the discomfort is so worth it when you get to the other side.

# THE Nudge

You feel the calling, you just know there's a book in you. It's that desire to write 'something', whether it's a well-crafted how-to book or the story of your life. It's right there and it's ready, waiting for you to hop on the back of inspiration and take a ride.

As a girl I was an avid reader, a bibliophile. I had this little spot in my playroom between a dresser and a bookcase, where if I sat just right I became invisible to the outside world. That little hidey-hole became a portal to different worlds - magic wardrobes, stuffed animals who came to life, mysteries to solve, epic journeys to undertake, secret gardens and princesses who did more than wait to be rescued (and some who just waited).

It was in that hidey-hole that I first felt the nudge. Grabbing the most imaginative book I could find, Alice in Wonderland, I sat down at my little typewriter and fed paper into it… click clack click clack - dutifully pretending, not to dive into the world of Wonderland, but pretending that I created it. Click clack and a little illustration - I followed the nudge I had inside to create something magical.

That nudge to paint a story became the need to write in a journal.

Books filled with my random thoughts and rants and profound insights.

Books filled with things that I felt the nudge to record, express, let out, create.

I received nudges for many 'real' books too. 15 to be exact.

But it's not enough to be nudged is it?

It's easy to ignore.

*It's easy to find other things more urgent, more persistent, more important than simply following a nudge.*

Until the nudge is no longer a nudge. It's a need.

My nudges had been shelved for long enough, and were in need of some serious attention.

My nudge to write a book became a non-negotiable need when I realized that 'Your Inner Council' was ready to be written. It wasn't just ready, it was pestering me - that beautiful concept kept hitting me in the back, deepening with every day. I started experiencing every chapter, every section, each of

the individual council members I held within me –
they all showed up in my life, one at a time, in my
face until I committed them to paper.

I was living my book in the same way I experienced those magical realms in my hidey-hole. Click-
ity-clack… it had to come out.

One of my clients wrote this to me just before coming out to my writing retreat… "So when I say this
is the worst possible time, so inconvenient, for me
to decide to write an actual BOOK and PUBLISH it – I
mean it. I have no business being on this plane, going to this retreat. But I can't not go. And that's
my cue. It's time. All these years, I considered
writing a book a luxury I couldn't afford. Something
people do who have time and money. Now I know better. Finally."

*That moment when it changes from 'some-
day' to 'it must come out' is the day when
becoming an author becomes real. That's the
time to dive in and write.*

# THE

Once I accepted that indeed the book was not going to leave me alone until it was written, my honeymoon period began.

In a frenzy of creativity I pulled out my journal and started the sketches. The big vision of what this book was and where it was going all poured out. Colored pens soiling the virgin paper, merging together to make something that no one had created before.

This was no Alice in Wonderland copy. This was me being a real, grown up author.

Once we, as authors, have accepted our fate and answered the demand of an idea we need to share, the creativity Gods shower us with ideas, book titles, chapter headings. We start writing chapters in our heads, in the shower or while we are driving or doing the dishes, and we start carrying a little notebook with us to jot down inspirations. That Word document is opened up and there it is - it's official.

*We are going to be writing the glorious book that clearly we've been called to write. It's fate and we're on a creative high.*

I don't know about you, but I was aware that my honeymoon period wasn't going to last forever. I was aware that this love affair with the idea of a book and the start of something so damn exciting would wane. So when it comes, when that juicy inspiration is ready to be picked, be prepared to ride the creativity wave for all it's worth, and use that extra juju for the good of your book to continuously fuel you through the entire creative process.

# FRESH

Get yourself a new fresh journal, one where every thought and action and little quotation about this book goes. It is a sacred container.

*Because there are times you need to draw, jot something down, map out an idea or write by hand instead of type or speak. And it doesn't need to be mixed up with all the other thousand things you need to jot down.*

Everyone that comes to my retreat is given a sketchbook on Day 1. Every time we talk, someone grabs a pen and starts writing down our magic words in that book. Little gems and clues pop onto the pages, some vital and some superfluous. It doesn't matter. If it's about the book, it goes into the journal with many colored pens.

To be clear, this is a free standing book specifically for this creation. You don't need to fill it, but keep it separate from your other thoughts and musing and notes.

I like big journals with no lines, sketch books with space.

But get the one that calls to you.

Label the spine with the title.

Because then it feels official.

It changes everything to have a dedicated space just for this one project...focused and contained, ready to be filled.

# WHO IS YOUR  *Reader?*

Most people start visualizing their book at the beginning of the reader's journey. What are their pain points? What do they need solved? That's logical. A to B to C.

I don't play that way.

Because nothing matters outside of who the reader is going to BE at the end of the book.

*What's shifted for them? What actions are they taking? Who have they become?*

I tell my coaching clients all the time that it'd be great if their businesses grew as a result of us working together, but my highest and greatest dream for them is that they develop the deepest sense of self-trust that they've ever had. And when I keep that in the forefront of every piece of copy and everything we talk about, what ends up happening is exactly that. Not only are the people who are drawn to work with me totally in alignment with my mission, they also 'get' that that's where we are going and it's infused into their system.

The end result becomes the flavoring for everything I do before we even start working together.

So let me ask you that same question…

Who is your reader when they put down your book?

I don't care about demographics or psychographics or any of the things most people who help you write books ask you. Who will they ideally be and where do you want them to go next is the most important piece of the map.

## They have finished reading your book and something changed for them. What is it?

This kind of backwards planning, or reverse engineering, is so powerful because now, everything you do has a litmus test. "Is this helping them BE ____?" becomes the mantra before you even start writing. Start at the end to see what picture you most need to paint.

# BACK END

So we've reverse engineered the energetics for your readers, now let's do the same for you. What is the highest and greatest outcome for your book?

Dream big here…be scared.

Now let's take this one step further…because the big dreams are fulfilled by taking small steps.

## *What is the next step you want the reader to take with YOU?*

Do you want them to buy another copy for their friend?

Do you want them to sign up for your email list?

Do you want them to enroll in a course? Come to an event?

Do you want them to spend thousands of dollars working with you?

Do you want them to beg you to speak at their event?

Do you want them to become a card carrying member of the change you wish to create in the world and to march with you?

Whatever it is, don't treat this book as a business card (I hate those kinds of books), but remember where you're going next. Add a few subtle clues and perhaps a few obvious ones. 'Your Inner Council' has an ad in the front and the back that asks the reader to go and download the companion workbook, adding them to my list. I also talk about coaching and my clients as part of my storytelling merely to plant the seeds (I'll talk more about seeding in the second section on writing).

One of my clients had done a TedX talk and sat down to write a book about the same topic. We went through the whole talk, the stories and the slide-show, until she came to the end, the call to action. She admitted that her call to action in the talk was weak. So as we fleshed out her book, she understood that her call to action truly was to get entrepreneurs and leaders of industry to take action in the world of learning and education.

In her business that meant hiring her as a consultant to get projects like this started. So the entire book was reframed and reorganized to make that section the culmination of the whole book, each piece leading to her readers becoming invested in the future of our youth. This could not have happened without understanding what her highest and best desire for the book would be.

*Don't just write the book. Write the book as a part of your overarching message to the world.*

Use this book as a way to connect with other people, for them to get to know you, understand you, want to be with you more. Use your book as a way of truly being able to say, "Here I am and this is what I stand for. Join me."

# HOW CAN YOU *Grow?*

So continuing on that thought, my next question is: how can YOU grow in the writing of this book?

We get so caught up in the idea that this book will change others that we lose sight of how you as a person need to grow to produce this body of work. When we place the transformation outside of ourselves, it becomes harder and harder to really connect with what we're writing.

But give a self-help junkie a reason to grow and explore more?

Now we're talking.

Because we can't take our readers anywhere we aren't willing to go first.

## So where are you going?

How are the lessons and stories in your book impacting you and your world?

Who do you want to be when you pick up that published book for the first time?

Because you will transform simply in the completion...

You will transform in the writing of your book...

You will transform simply by starting your book.

Writing a book is the most impact filled piece of self-growth I (and my clients) ever move through. It transforms our own self-worth and how we view our ability to create in the world.

It refines our vision and forces us to put a stake in the ground that says, 'this is who I am and this is the change I wish to impart upon the world'.

*Writing a book means we get to find the core of our message and we get to share the stories that will best express that. We get to be brave enough to share ourselves in a seemingly permanent way.*

Every person who writes a book has at least one moment of panic (or 5,153), one place where we have a choice to dive in deeper into our vulnerability, into our message and our beliefs, or to turn away, give up, hide our brightest light.

And every published author has had the strength of character to go beyond that discomfort and create something that would not have existed without their leap of faith.

This is your journey into growth if you choose to see it as such.

Take the opportunity and dive in.

# ARE YOU A CONTENT *hoarder?*

If you're driven to express yourself through writing then you've probably already written or spoken a ton of things in the world that you now have a chance to reclaim.

This undeniable need to use words as paint shows up in emails, Facebook posts, videos, call recordings, live talks, blogs, journals, even notes from conversations with clients.

Imagine everywhere you've ever written or spoken.

ALL of it is content, sitting there, used once and forgotten.

While you can argue that it wasn't hoarded, that it was shared, I disagree. Did that message reach everyone it was meant to reach?

*Hoarding is the "excessive acquisition and an inability or unwillingness to discard large quantities of objects".*

We just keep creating...not truly honoring the message that has come out. We keep piling more and more content on top of content. I have a client who has written a blog post every week for 10 years. Another who has had a podcast for 8 years and has written a blog for nearly as long. Another who has emailed her list weekly for 6 years. And another who has had coaching conversations with clients for 4 years.

All of these content creators just keep creating without pausing to truly reflect on what has been created already.

It just keeps piling up, rarely revisited.

Add the desire to create a book on top of it all?

It's quite possible that you my friend, like me, are a classic over-creator. Always seeking that new expression, the next piece of content to create, the next project. In our wake lies a sea of words waiting to be noticed.

So we start here first. Before we need to type one word in our book, let's see what you've already created before we try to create something entirely new and different".

# BE A *Collector*

Nothing beats paper. Nothing.

Faced with the printouts of her body of work that was over a foot tall, my client realized that there were several books already written. In fact a small series of books could be edited and published pretty easily. She also found the foundation of a powerful course ready to roll.

All amongst the pile of writing she had produced and set aside.

Another client had pages of content set aside from all of his client sessions, full of insights and thoughts. Piled together suddenly he could see what men were hiring him for. He could see his own story woven into theirs. And his book was born, downloaded over 1,000 times in the first day.

For me, I write on Facebook. Somehow that platform has become home to my morning musings, the thoughts that drift by are captured and channelled into little posts. My blog ignored, I realized that I was indeed creating content every day. My assistant now 'stalks' me on Facebook, gathering all my posts on my profile and in the groups I manage (speaking of which, make sure you join my writing group at facebook.com/writethedamnbook). She turns those posts into blog posts and then the real magic happens… she puts them all into a word document.

...and then I print them out on paper.

## Because nothing beats seeing your writing in front of you.

When I started the book 'Active Surrender' I went through those piles, and 143 pages of the book was written instantly. Half the content of the book was found in the things I had already written.

Yes, I edit and weave those stories more tightly into the book but the point is, you have content leaking out in the world everywhere.

## It's time to collect it all. Gather it all up. Transcribe it. Copy and paste it. Pile up the notes and journals. Print it. On real paper.

Listen, some of you will be thinking that it would take just too much paper, that it's a waste of resources. Well consider this - it's a waste of creativity to be hoarding this artwork away. THAT's a waste of resources. Buy recycled paper if it soothes your soul, but there is something so profound in seeing your body of work in front of you. It is not

only super helpful to find themes but it's also a
big awakening to those who always feel like they
have to create more, only to have it wither away
somewhere on their computer.

Be a reformed hoarder starting today.

Make those piles and we'll play with them.

# NOT QUITE A *Hoarder?*

Okay so maybe you haven't been as addicted to writing and speaking as many of my clients, or me for that matter. That's fine because there's another way to collect.

And it's all about you.

What are your stories?

What are your lessons?

## *What are you brilliant at?*

What do you suck at?

Don't go writing all of these stories right now, just start making a list - get titles or memory prompts down on paper.

You may be writing a book about something totally unrelated to you (or so you think), but do this anyway. Because there's nothing better than stories about you infused into your book.

*The reader wants you. Wants to know what you know, wants to hear your challenges and your 'stuff'.*

You may not have been hoarding your writing but if you haven't shared your own personal journey then that makes you a hoarder of stories, right?

Get those down without judgement or thought. Start thinking of times in your life where you found yourself on a journey. Start to see the lessons you've learned. Start to see the lessons you still need to learn. Whatever they are, write them down.

# DON'T FORGET *The Map*

You can skip everything I've said so far, but do your best to stop here and act.

Listen, I know it's very much a high school flashback for you to create an outline. But it changes everything to create the most robust outline you can possible create.

'Your Inner Council' was written 3 times before it was published.

The first time I had created a general pathway… 9 council members and who they were. That was it. I wrote and wrote but something was missing.

The second time, I went back and collected my stories and inserted them. Something was still missing.

The third time happened months later. My book languished and I agonized over what was wrong with it. I had set it aside. I resigned myself to a book that just wasn't finishing.

Until I sat down and created a visual map. I started laying out the stories I had included, along with the basic structure. There was the introduction which actually had several different sections and then the nine council members, each with their own stories.

As I sat there looking at the map, I noticed distinct holes, areas where what I truly wanted to say wasn't being said. I saw where some areas had ten stories and others had two. I saw all of the missing pieces. I also saw where some stories needed to be eliminated completely, were stuck in the wrong place or even, in some cases, the wrong book entirely. So I kept putting more and more details into the map, drawing mountains and rivers and little towns until the whole book was there in front of me.

## *Had I created that map in round one, I could have saved myself nearly 6 months of supposed writer's block.*

I was working with a client at a retreat. She had already created a course and had an outline available but as we dove into the outline for the book, an entirely different book came out, one that was even more focused than the course, one that went deeper into three distinct areas instead of the 24 from her course.

Now here's the thing for her - she loves writing and is a natural story teller, but she gets lost in the writing. To see an entire book all the way through was just overwhelming.

The map we created not only gave the clarity of distilling the 24 into three; it also gave her a consistent container for each of the topics, breaking them each into three subsections, each of those with a discussion, a story, a poem and a quote. Suddenly a huge task of writing a Book with a capital 'B' became writing nine stories with some context.

Another client could grasp the intellectual process of making a map but was so filled with information and facts that I sent her off with 200 index cards. She filled every single one of them with individual topics. 200 pieces of data that she wanted to put into a small 100 page book that would be read in an hour. Allowing her to brain dump on the cards gave us access to one gaping void…

Ultimately, she wanted her book to be a call to action, which meant she needed people to become enrolled in her movement. But there's nothing enrolling about facts. She needed to add stories. So when we created her map we pulled out the big paper and we started with a story for each section. We asked 'what is the story here' first, and then 'are there one or two facts that help to support that story'? 'Is there a discussion this can open up'? In doing so, it became obvious that the first two sections would very brief (the information heavy sections) and the second two sections would be filled with stories and examples supporting that enrollment process.

The map makes all the difference.

## *It's not the sexy work.*

My clients at the end of the first day of my retreats always look brain-worn and anxious…will they
ever get to start writing?

Of course! So stick it out.

Because when we take the time to really outline
where you're going, the journey you will be taking
people on, we find things that we didn't know we
were missing. We find new pathways that feel even
juicier. We sometimes change the entire direction
of the book.

I had a client realize that who she thought she
was writing to was not who she really wanted to
work with, so the voice of the book needed to be
completely different. Because she realized this as
a part of the mapping process, she saved herself
months of writing the WRONG book.

This is where your head and heart most need to com-
municate because the container you build sets the
tone for the entire creative process.

# INDEX CARDS, BIG PAPER AND *Journals*

Your map doesn't need to be done in a certain way. You're creative, so create a structure that feels really good. Each different project has demanded that I create a different kind of structure.

I used a very visual map for 'Your Inner Council', drawing out what each section would look and feel like because it made the project fun.

For 'Unconventional Wisdom', a more traditional linear outline (like we used in school) worked just fine to make sure all the stories were in their proper order.

For 'Active Surrender', I blocked out 4 pages per section, each with the same purpose so that each of the 7 sections got mapped out in the same way.

This book? Old fashioned flash cards. I just started writing down each little idea on a separate card, shuffled them into 4 distinct sections and then put them in some order. As I write I've moved cards to other sections and yes, tossed out a couple and created a couple of new ones.

For my clients, we very often use everything. We have BIG paper with colored pens taped up on the walls. And then we talk it through and they write down the juicy gems in their journals. We go through hundreds of flashcards and have post-its stuck everywhere.

Mind maps. Movable parts. Big swirling arrows.

## Try them all.

Find the way that feels right for you.

A friend asked me to explain to him what my maps look like.

They look like as much fun as I can have doing brain work…

It doesn't matter what the map looks like, but don't start walking without one. The more details you can infuse into your map, the easier it is to simply open it up and insert words.

# STORY AND

Every book has a balance. There is a sweet spot where the form takes a very well-rounded feel. This is what the map will help you with.

*But here's the thing I most want you to remember...if you're teaching someone something, nothing is more important than using stories.*

And no story is as important as your own.

Ever.

There's this voice authors sometimes speak from at first which sounds a bit like lecturing, like a robot imparting great wisdom. But it's hard for a reader to want to engage in your wisdom if they can't relate to it. Story creates relatability effortlessly. Story allows the reader to see themselves in the information, to relate to big concepts and story allows them to feel like they know you.

Great religions start and end with story, because stories are powerful tools.

*So if you're busy creating a map that doesn't include stories, or only has one story at the beginning, you're missing an author's most powerful weapon.*

In order to really balance out your book, you must make sure that every concept has some form of story attached to it.

Don't skip your stories, because those make your book into a great builder of a relationship. That end result for the book you're going for? It can only happen if you're willing to clearly express who you are.

# READY? SET? *Sort*

So you've collected one big jumble of awesomeness, and some crap tossed in for good measure.

This is a step that is very revealing and inspiring.

Because now, we get to sort through all the piles.

I do this process with every client and it brings up different anxieties: that their material won't be enough, that there's too much to sort through, that what they have won't fit, that it'll be too much to really find all of the pieces.

*There are themes in what we create and what we do. Our lives have common threads woven into them, expressed without us truly knowing that those threads are always there.*

Pick up a note… what is it about? Start a pile or tag it with a post it sticking out on the side. As you go sifting through all of your writing, suddenly those threads start to GLOW.

If you know what book you're already writing, look for things that support where you're already going.

If you don't know what book you're writing, search for the topics that pop up the most. It will become obvious that perhaps you've written about, let's say, vulnerability 50 times and barely touched another topic.

When writing 'Your Inner Council' I had 9 distinct topics I thought I was searching for, but as I sorted, a couple of them changed, adjusted to the language I was already speaking into the world, honoring the words I'd already written.

As I collected stories for 'Active Surrender', I was only looking for stories on trust and surrender and I found 7 distinct subtopics hidden within those stories. At the same time, I also found almost an entire book on creating our businesses intuitively, which is a future book I will dive into, especially since it's almost written already.

*Allow the themes to unfold and present themselves to you. Allow your idea to be enriched or shifted by all of the content you've already surrounded yourself with.*

Keep making those piles and sifting for those juicy nuggets, the ones you can adjust or edit or include as-is. This will significantly cut down your writing time and will give you a very robust start to the entire project.

As a side note, I didn't do this step until the second draft of "Your Inner Council". My first draft didn't include any of my stories. It was all written from scratch and it wasn't quite right. I hadn't included any of my previous writing, and I was missing a lot of the insights my followers were craving. Once I went back and included those pieces I'd found lying around, the book took on a whole new life and became something much richer and more well-rounded. Now I don't even bother starting a book project without collecting and sorting first.

# YOUR NOT-SO TARGET *market*

This little piece is going to be contrary to how most book writing programs begin… you're told to find your target market and write to them.

I hate that advice.

## *Because I write for me.*

And quite frankly, I am my own target market.

See here's the thing – your writing is a little piece of your soul being recorded on the pages. We found themes in your writing because those are pieces of your soul scattered in words.

In non-fiction, whatever it is we're expressing comes from us, our lessons, our stories, the things we've learned.

I wrote 'Your Inner Council' for me, 10 years ago... the person who knew that I was intuitive but didn't really have a way of trusting my own voice, of tapping into my higher voice and listening. I was constantly seeking that next guru to help me find MY purpose and MY path. Had I known about my Inner Council then, I could have saved myself years of searching outside of myself and I would have started a more active dialogue with myself.

I wrote 'Active Surrender' because I had a year where I could do nothing BUT surrender. I experienced it every day and I fought it tooth and nail. But I found that when I did actually surrender, things happened, success came in larger proportions, my life unfolded beautifully. Had I learned that at the beginning of the year, how much energy could I have saved not fighting myself?

I wrote this book because I could have used a guide when I dreamed of being an author 15 times over before that first book got published.

I am my own target audience.

*Whether it is who I am now, or who I was last year, 10 years ago, as a child or who I will be next year or 10 years from now. It's all me.*

So if the words and the lessons resonate with ME and they teach ME, then I'm on the right track.

You are your target audience. If you're learning, so will they...

And I will add, that sometimes, if our target market is not us, it's still useful to think of it as us because somewhere in there is our story, the reason why we NEED to write this book. Our story is the undercurrent of everything we write. Claim that now.

# ONE MORE *Time*

Do not proceed with your book without a map, without knowing where you're going, without knowing who you want your reader to be in the end and without knowing who you want to be at the end… seriously.

I know a lot of writers who sit down to write a book a little each day without a map.

They just keep writing.

*It's a bit like following the car in front of you and trusting you'll get to where you're going. You might, but it's not always the most direct route.*

I'll add a side note here that as this book was being edited, my editor stuck a note on that last sentence that said "From personal experience, it's also a huge ballache to organize it into something coherent AFTER the fact!" Exactly...

Listen, I'm a deeply intuitive person.

I LOVE just showing up and seeing what happens.

And I also know the power of intention and how much clarity is required to really truly manifest something.

When you have a map it allows your writing time to be dedicated solely to writing. Not to thinking about what to write or getting in the mindset to write. You get to sit down, pick a topic and simply write. Your map allows you to write MORE intuitively because it takes the guesswork out, it alleviates the pressure on your grey matter that says 'what are we writing about today?' Sit down, pick a section that really appeals to you and go.

## Make it easy to succeed in this and set yourself up for writing awesomeness.

So stop here and find an inspiring way to give yourself as clear a vision for your book as possible. The map is your most important tool, not just for writing but for FINISHING the damn book.

# MONEY

Let's get this out...there are ideas about being an author that revolve around money. That authors can make millions. That you'll never make money on the book. That this needs to be a portal into other areas where you can make money. That you have to hustle to create income from this.

And all of those things are true.

## *And all of the opposite things about those things are also true.*

So let's take money off the table right now.

Because we make up enough stories about the book and what it will mean to us without having to add money to the landscape. Writing a book isn't about the money – but money can be a part of the plan. It can be a part of your strategy.

But until the book is written and published, it means nothing.

I have friends that make multiple six figures from book sales alone.

I have friends who have sold 27 copies of their book.

I have friends that make five, six and even seven figure incomes from speaking, coaching and related products because of their books.

I have friends who just love giving away the book and build nothing from it but satisfaction.

Money matters if you're a business person.

I personally love to look at my books as connectors, to connect my heart with other people's hearts. I hope some kind of inspiration or change happens for them as a result of the reading of my books.

And yes, I do make beautiful income on the back end of the books, but I don't focus on sales and I don't focus on the leverage.

Numbers aren't my personal driver.

*I just write the best damn books I can, and I love on my people, and the business comes. My money mindset is automatically trusting that money loves me and loves coming to me.*

And yes, a book does bring up the fear that the author will never make money on this book, so why are they spending all this time and these resources to create one? And that's a mindset shift. Shift to the beauty of creation, both of this book and of the financial win that is coming. Then release it. Release the pressure to make the book succeed. Release the expectation of millions.

It could happen.

But it doesn't matter right now.

Right now set the big dream, and then release it into the world so you can focus on what's most important – which is writing the damn book.

One more money note...Some people feel that the only way to make money as an author is to have a publisher who gets your book into book stores. This was the norm even 10 years ago. However, I personally know authors who make bank BECAUSE they aren't in a traditional publishing relationship. I also know people who paid a publisher to produce their work and they've yet to see a substantial commission check.

The money you create from being an author is based on YOU and what you choose to do with that book and how you decide to share your book with the world, which of course you can only do when you've actually written the damn book. So yes, have a plan and a vision for the money creation and do the inner money mindset work to prepare yourself, and keep writing.

# WRITING

# HOW *Powerful* IS YOUR NEED TO WRITE THAT *Book*?

You've done all the background work and visioning so now it's time to start the actual writing.

Listen, on any given day I can think of 1,034 reasons why I don't have time to write the book or why I'm not ready. I'm in a lot of writing groups and those who are actually making progress are a pittance compared to those who dream of it. I have people messaging me all the time saying that they have a book in them but they haven't started yet for X-Y-Z reasons.

I've done the stats in writing groups in those moments where my Virgo goes wild... Only 2 out of 37 people are actually working on their book in earnest. The rest dabble, or get stuck before they even start.

Why? Because while there are 1,034 reasons not to work on it, there's only one reason to write it... because you NEED to.

I know that with me, it became something I thought about almost daily. I kept feeling that nudge until it became a kick. It kept hanging over my head, waiting, showing me where I wasn't following through. It drained my energy.

When the reasons not to write become quieter than the reason to write, then we can play.

You choose your pace.

But for crying out loud stop holding onto your message like it's a mountain. Writing a book doesn't have to be hard work people... but you have to make that ONE commitment to writing it.

Ready?

# TIME TO GET DOWN TO *Writing* NOW RIGHT?

Time to get serious. This writing thing is going to be magical and you're going to be super structured with it.

You're determined to write for an hour a day.

You've committed to 1,000 words a day.

One full chapter day after day.

You've blocked out writing time on your calendar.

And it works for the first couple of days, maybe even a week.

Then one hour turns into 'maybe I'll get to it later'.

1,000 words turns into 100 here and there.

A chapter? Maybe just a page today… Oh those clients totally trump that writing time on the calendar so let's just cross that off now.

Sound familiar?

## Then the fears creep in… making all that time scheduling and setting goals for your writing feel so much less sexy.

So right now, write yourself a permission slip. Permission to not set yourself up with a system that you know is going to fail. Permission to be flexible with your creative flow. Flexibility doesn't mean absence of action, just a bit more intuitive flow in the actions you do take.

I'll talk more about consistency and fears and different ways to make this whole book writing thing easier, but for now I beg you, don't promise yourself an hour a day if you like a flexible schedule, don't promise yourself x-many words each day if you have no real idea how many words you can comfortably write.

## In other words - don't make promises you probably won't keep.

Because it undermines your self-trust and authoring a book already stretches those trust muscles to the max. You don't need more reasons to quit.

You're creative.

## *Let's think creatively.*

Let's find ways to keep writing that support us and feel anything other than confining…

Let's get writing.

# YOUR *Lover*

Sometimes we think of writing our book as a job, as this thing we 'must' do each day. Clock in. Clock out. It's due to the editor by this date so I need to write this many words each day, and so on.

*Thinking of your book as a job is stressful and takes the joy out of writing.*

Imagine instead that you welcome your book as a lover, a long distance lover that you get to be on vacation with. You go on a one month trip to a private island to be intimate and loving, to lay hands on each other, touching, laughing, being with one another, hot sand beneath your bodies, being caressed by a gentle salty breeze.

You would take advantage of every second of that trip because you crave that connection. You wouldn't ignore your lover. You would talk about what you want, your desires, your dreams. You would make time for each other and look forward to every second. You would welcome them in your arms, limbs tangled, the separation from one body to the next disappearing.

It's not a job.

It's not something trackable.

*You can give yourself a timeline to complete your book and not have it feel restrictive.*

Because your book can be treated with the enthusiasm and passion and love that you would treat a lover. Enter into the writing space as if your toes just stepped off of that plane onto the sunny beach; a secret tryst you can't wait to get to.

# THAT
## *Consistency*
# THING

3 days.

That's about as long as I last on any challenge.

At one point I thought about creating a series of 3 day challenges, but I didn't make it past GoDaddy and a concept.

Consistency isn't my superpower.

Or my secret weapon.

Or even part of my vocabulary.

It's actually kind of my nemesis.

Which was exactly the challenge in writing a full grown-up book.

Wayne Dyer used to get up early every morning, go into his office and write and write and write. Every day. So surely I could do that. I love writing. Every day seemed doable.

Until day 3.

Then it started to feel like work. So the next few pages are dedicated to those who aren't hustlers, for whom long distance running isn't a thing. And for those who want to find different ways of having flow in your projects, there's a magic trick… because it isn't about consistency.

## It's about love and attention.

I don't need to be consistent – because it's not who I am.

It's who other people are and goddess-bless-them-mofos.

But it's not me…

And I've still managed to publish my books.

*Because my books don't need consistency, they just need attention in whatever form that takes. We water our plants and feed our children and take showers. We give love and attention to our spouses and friends.*

Why not turn that on our books?

This is a relationship, not a project. This is breathing life into something that doesn't exist without that breath.

It can languish and wither away.

Or it can grow and evolve.

It doesn't take much but it does take an open hearted connection to what we're creating all of the time.

## So don't worry about being consistent.

Wonder if you've given a moment of energy and attention to what you're growing.

# 3 MINUTE *Practice*

Part of the problem with being consistent with authoring a book is that we get overly ambitious with our schedules. We start blocking off big chunks of our schedule and words sometimes take a long time to come through. It takes longer than we think we have time for. We need time to get in the mood to write.

It becomes a black hole in our day and so we avoid it.

We put other things in front of it.

*But if we go back to the energy and love piece, we can get it out of our heads that we have to schedule ourselves tons of time.*

What if we only had 3 minutes each day? Whenever those 3 minutes land is right and perfect.

My friend was on non-stop calls all day but he committed to writing a little bit every day, so after the kids went to bed he kicked out 300 words. He found a few minutes to pound on the keyboard just a little.

Swimming around in your book for 3 minutes a day helps you move forward, even if 3 minutes is all you've got. Time is never the real issue we don't write, because everyone can find time if they truly want to.

*Those 3 minutes are magical for me because they remind me that I love writing. I almost never truly feel like not writing.*

I get to choose where to focus my gifts and for 3 minutes, my friends, we can choose to journal about the book, outline it, meditate on it, write in it, or even edit it.

Some days I'm done after 3 minutes.

And some days, I get so into writing that 3 hours pass.

But my book craves just that little touch of energy.

# THE 30 MINUTE Sprint

"But when I write I disappear for hours…" she tells me on Day 3 of the retreat.

So I reply, "That is exactly the problem. It's exactly why you haven't already written your book, because you don't have time to write for hours every day. So you don't write at all."

And there's a pause, the one that says 'damn you'…

Because there are 2 ways to look at 30 minutes. The first is that it sounds like a long time. The second is that it's not enough.

For most authors sitting down for 30 minutes is barely enough time to even get into writing. They sit there for a while and think about what to write, and where they want to go. And then the fingers start warming up a little. Lots of thinking happens before we allow our creativity to flow out of us.

*But when you've worked on your map and it's gorgeous and beautiful, 30 minutes is easy - because you don't have to think about what to write. You get to look at the map and just start writing.*

You get to dive straight into creativity.

But here's where it get tricky. Because at 30 minutes the timer goes off. And you might be in the middle of something awesome. And that's the perfect place to pause.

Make a note of where you were going.

Get up.

Stretch.

Go to the bathroom.

Get a drink.

Why? Because training yourself to not get lost in the creation helps your brain NOT have the excuse of 'I don't have hours to spend today so I won't write at all.' If you train yourself to pause every 30 minutes you can learn to dive in faster and separate faster when you need to do other things. We spend all of the third day of my retreats putting the timer on in 30 minute increments specifically to help the flow KEEP going.

Because if you write until the creative thought dies, then your creativity dries up and you have to walk away for longer periods of time to replenish it. But when you walk away while it's hot...after few minutes you can't wait to get back to writing. It's like hearing the siren song of your computer calling you to start typing again...

*Sprint for 30 minute increments and you'll find that not only is your creativity lit, it will be lit for longer and you will no longer be limited by the idea that writing a book needs to dominate your life.*

Also, on the flip side, knowing that you have a break coming in 30 minutes allows your brain to not wander off for a quick Facebook check or an email reply. You can wait just a few more minutes until the timer goes off, which inevitably helps your flow.

# THE 24 HOUR *Book*

My book was dying. It had gone through two full rounds of rewrites and then nothing for six months. Not even three minutes was going to get me re-engaged.

I got super excited when I went back and redid my book map and made it really robust and juicy. I knew exactly what I needed to write.

But I still wasn't writing it.

I'm not a long distance runner… I get bored, I get distracted, I'm not consistent enough. But I'm a GREAT sprinter. I understand that I can kick butt for short spurts and then I can relax until the next sprint comes along.

So why not approach this third and final re-write that way?

Why not use that short-term mentality to my advantage?

So I gave myself an impossible deadline… 24 hours to send off my final copy to my creative editor.

It was due to her by 5:00 pm on Friday afternoon.

I sent it at 3:37 pm.

Yes, I got a full night's sleep and yes, I ate. But for the most part I sat at my desk, Facebook OFF, writing away, filling in those stories I'd identified on my new outline. 30 minute Pomodoro's all day long. I had such a robust map that I just went through it checking off things that needed re-wording, changing stories that needed rewriting and adding in the missing pieces.

My fingers felt like they were going to fall off.

## But I finished the damn book in a sprint.

Not consistently or over time...in one fell swoop.

Add up all those hours I was TRULY writing the book, minus the distractions and the bathroom breaks and the quick emails and you'll find that it doesn't take nearly as long as we think to write the damn book when we actually do it.

# PEAS UNDER THE
## *Mattress*

The Princess and the Pea was one of my favorite books as a young girl for no other reason than that it led to so many unanswerable questions. Like was the pea cooked or dried? How did so many mattresses stay put all night? Did she have a ladder? Why was a princess from so far away walking around the rain in the middle of the night? Were there no guards at the gate? And so on…

In other words, the book itself led to a series of peas under my mattress as I got more and more distracted from the storyline as I read the book.

Sitting down, even for just 3 minutes, is filled with peas.

*Little tiny insignificant things will pull you away from writing.*

Sometimes that's okay. Sometimes it's unacceptable.

Distractions happen.

In writing just this little piece on peas, I've checked a message that came in, I've rearranged what index card comes next, I've called my son's doctor to check on a referral, and I've gotten up to get some water.

Peas happen.

There will be days when your concentration is amazing.

And there will be days when it's scattered all over the place.

That's okay.

Don't fight the pea.

Notice it, take care of it and then get back to writing that next sentence.

*The more I allow the peas to just happen without beating myself up for them, the less they truly distract me from writing.*

I'd love to give you advice like I've heard, to remove distractions and shut them all down and place yourself in a void… but that's impractical for most of us. The idea that to write we must be in a per-

fect state of solace with lots of time just gives us
another reason not to write.

We've got a bowlful of peas sitting here on our desk
that look pretty fun to play with.

Distractions are a part of life.

Learn to be okay with them and more flexible with
your creativity and you'll find it easier to actually
BE creative.

# I DON'T *Feel* LIKE IT

'I don't feel like it' and 'it's not calling to me' are an intuitive's best excuse. I don't always feel like doing things. I'm essentially lazy. And sometimes (I KNOW I'm not alone here...) I use that as the reason I'm not doing certain things, like writing my book. Okay, it's usually the reason I use for not writing my book.

*I know my book projects are aligned and ready and are simply waiting for me to take movement towards creating them...and 'I don't feel like it' isn't really true.*

Perhaps I don't want to take on something really big. A book is a big thing. Well, what if I took the tiniest step, just one thing that is simple and easy?

Perhaps the details that have to be done bore me. A book is filled by just sitting there cranking out the words for an idea and vision we had. Can't get much more detail-y than that right? Well, what if I wrote out of order, found that chapter or story I've been really wanting to write and I wrote that instead of the next linear piece?

Perhaps the potential outcome scares me. The idea of having to market the book, of having other people read and critique my work, the nakedness of having my words on display...those things are all hypothetical futures that are scary. Well what if living in the future isn't going to help me today?

Perhaps I want to watch a movie instead of write? Well what if I wrote AND watched the movie?

Perhaps I'm already on to the next pretty shiny idea. Well what if I spent 3 minutes on the existing project before playing with the next?

*ALIGNED ACTION IS NOT ALWAYS GLAMOROUS OR FEEL-GOODY. And as intuitives we know we simply can't make ourselves do the things we don't want to do... so find the balance. Find the small things that will tip your writing back into feeling right and perfect.*

This book, this journey, it's important. Don't set it aside because you don't feel like working on it. Give it love and attention and then go do what's calling you next.

# INTRODUCTIONS *First*

Where do you begin writing your book? At the beginning of course.

Your introduction is the container for your book so it's a gorgeous place to get started. It's also sometimes the most daunting, so let's just rip that Band-Aid off now. The book really can be written in any order you want if you have a map of what's going into it.

But the introduction is the part that drives some of my clients into breakdown mode and gets some of my clients incredibly excited.

## *So it's exactly why we start writing here.*

Here's the truth about that introduction piece – it's the one piece of writing that will change the most as you write the book. Use it as a first round place-holder. I guarantee that as you write, more pieces will start falling into place. I guarantee that the introduction will be added to, edited, scrapped and rewritten more times than any other part of your book. Because it is where you get to really set up the whole container. And the more your write, the deeper the container will become, and the water within that container will start taking on other colors.

## So write the introduction first.

And expect that it's not really the true introduction, merely the start of the book as a whole. A place to put your foot down and say - okay. Let's do this.

# WRITE SHIT.
# CHANGE THE *World*

I published a digital magazine for 2 years. It came out on the 1st of every month and every single month I would write my article last. In fact I'd wait until the magazine had to go out to write it. And every month I'd message my best friend and say, "my article really sucked this month but hey, the magazine had to go out so I published it anyway."

And every month I'd get messages from people about how something in my article shifted things for them or how much they loved it. There were people who always read my article first because they looked forward to reading it month after month.

*I wrote what I thought was shit and I changed the world, one person at a time.*

I was insecure. I didn't know if it made any sense. I didn't know if anyone would get anything from my story or from my insights. But it didn't matter, because those who did get it, who did gain value, made it all worthwhile.

## So before you start judging what you're writing, don't.

Write shit.

Hit publish.

Change the world.

# WRITE

"Write drunk. Edit sober." - Hemingway.

While I've never actually written a book while drunk (although we do actually drink a good deal of wine at my retreats), the point is to write with abandon. Write like you can't physically stop yourself. Write without filters. Say it the way you really want to say it, not how you think you should say it.

Don't posture or position your writing. Don't edit it. Don't censure it.

## Write drunk.

Those things you most want to speak but wouldn't when you're trying to be proper and author-y? Write that.

Put it all down. Things can be edited, removed, added, spell-checked later.

Just write.

Be wild and creative and uncontained.

Channel your inner wisdom.

Be grammatically improper.

Mix up its and it's.

Use one sentence paragraphs.

Use no commas. Or too many commas.

Don't capitalize.

Write in all CAPS.

*It doesn't matter... it only matters that you're writing with heart and soul. Stripped down to your truth, trusting that every bump can be smoothed out later.*

Write drunk.

# SIFT FOR *Gold*

Edit sober… during the writing process you don't need to concern yourself with editing. But sometimes during my 3 minutes I simply go back and read what I've written as a way of finding out where I am.

And in those moments, I sift for gold.

*Because invariably there will be a thought that drifted into the drunken writing that stands out, that's pure gold.*

Pull it out.

Does it want more to be built around it? Sometimes it's a whole new section or chapter in that rambling thought. Sometimes it so perfectly expresses what I meant that I delete most of the other words.

This isn't editing - don't get distracted by that yet. But I do feel that it's important for me to keep a pulse on what I've written and make adjustments to the map as needed.

In 'Active Surrender' I found this juicy little nugget that talked about the duality of trust, to trust both sides of love, giving and receiving. And suddenly I saw that in each different topic, I needed to add the topic's counterpart to really round out those trust muscles. Without seeing that little nugget of gold, I would have missed a majorly awesome piece of the puzzle and the book would have felt somehow incomplete, like I missed something really juicy.

So from time to time, on one of those days you don't 'feel' like writing, go sifting for gold and see what comes up.

And sometimes the gold is the book itself... you see that what you're writing is really pretty amazing.

# WRITE FOR *You*

You know all those fears that pop up around publishing a book? There is a secret tip that I want to share with you now that negates almost every single 'Who am I to write a book' and all of the 'What if people hate it' things that wiggle their way into our process.

It's a simple shift in how you write… see most people get distracted by their work being out in the world, by the idea that their work is to help others.

That's a great altruistic way of being.

But what if this book is for you?

## What if you were writing for you?

What would you write if you were in your bed, scribbling in your journal, the smell of morning coffee wafting by, feeling the warmth of the covers wrapped around your legs?

Would it matter if it wasn't good enough?

*What are you learning about you, your process, your own self-development, your stories in the process of writing this book?*

During the writing process, you are the audience and the recipient of knowledge and insight.

Editing will help ensure others will understand you.

But in the creation cycle, focus on writing just for you.

When you do, you'll notice that all those fears simply drift away. You may be your own worst critic, but in this moment allow this book to be an extension of your own self-discovery.

# BE YOUR *Message*

Listen, you don't have to be perfect. You don't have to know everything. You don't have to be an expert. You don't even have to have years and years and years of experience.

And you don't have to pretend that you are perfect.

Write from where you are, because wherever that is, it's a step or two ahead of someone else.

## *Walk the path. Be your message.*

And lead honestly from where you are right now.

Also remember that what you're writing now may not apply to you in a year or five years or ten. But it will always apply to that person who is a step or two behind you right now.

Just write from where you are.

Being your message is the most powerful place you can come from.

# BECAUSE IT'S
*Scary*

At a certain point in any writing adventure, the voices come.

And while writing for me works, there's also another piece that helps me to continue through my doubts. It's that little piece inside of me that says – yeah, this is scary and that's exactly why I've got to keep going.

When I was writing this book, I started really wondering why I was writing it. I was posting up in the Writing The Damn Book Facebook Group about my daily progress and I hit a speedbump on Day 5 so I came clean...

"It's not complicated or long (I don't even think I'll get to 100 pages) but I feel like it's complete enough to get people moving on their books from start to finish. I just want people to write, not hide behind reading an instruction book before their hands start scribbling... a part of me feels like it's not going to be enough, like I want to justify it. I can hear the criticisms: "wow you really didn't put much time into it because you're writing it so fast". Or, "is that all"? Or, "there are so many other books with way more meat on them", and so on.

But I'll just keep writing and see what happens. No point projecting myself to the end of the project when I'm smack dab in the middle."

I share this because we all have things pop up. This writing process, whether it's personal or informational, is vulnerable. I've published books and I still feel that fear and self-doubt pop up.

But it just doesn't matter.

*Because at the end of the day, we can choose to keep writing what will possibly suck and possibly not, or we can choose to quit, to keep dreaming of the day where we are good enough to write the damn book.*

Little hint...being ready is a lie. We're never ready. If it's not scary, we're not writing.

Sit back down and write.

# Seeding

There is nothing more offensive to me than picking up a book and seeing nothing but ads and links. I sat down to read a book just the other day that literally had 4 links to the author's site and programs in the first chapter alone. I had to stop reading it even though there were some great juicy nuggets in there.

So yes, I encourage you to have a plan of where your readers are going next. And I want you to understand how you can seed your book powerfully without being spammy.

Write your book just how you want to in the first round. Add your stories. Add stories about clients and friends and about you. Now go back through it - not for editing but for planting seeds. Change little things.

One of my clients wanted to get more speaking engagements and saw the book as a great way to do that. So throughout the book we started seeding - adding little pieces of 'when I spoke at…' or 'I was standing there on stage…' These shifts in how she was demonstrating a point or telling a story helped the reader know without a doubt that this woman is a speaker, and based on the story, a damn good one at that. She wasn't coming out saying 'hire me here' on every other page, but she was planting that seed in the reader's consciousness that they want to hear her speak.

Be supportive in your seeding. If you read your seeding as a client would, is it a 'hit over the head' message or does it create that desire and knowing and positioning. It's a fine line but one that's really great to walk because it makes the book experience richer for the reader if they know there is more to learn afterwards.

*You have a plan for your reader's next steps. Find ways that feel good to infuse that as you write. Shoot! You'll see it in this book. Study how I've done it, where I do it, what it feels like to see or hear those seeds for you as the reader.*

Don't assume your reader knows that they want to hire you or buy your course or take that next step with you, whatever it looks like. Be clear and intentional with your seed planting so that if they are so driven, they know exactly what to do after reading your book.

# FIND YOUR *Voice*

The reason I rejected the first draft of 'Your Inner Council' is because I hated how I sounded. There was this stupid idea planted somewhere in the back of my mind that in order to write an acceptable spiritual book I had to go all airy-fairy-goddessy.

There's nothing wrong with airy-fairy-goddessy.

It's just not me or who I am.

I make up words and I'm a bit sassy. My spiritual essence is pretty grounded and practical. And yep, I tend to pepper my speech with the occasional swear word.

So the book sounded nothing like me. I was using a voice that I thought I needed to sound like to show I was qualified to write in this particular genre.

The second draft wasn't much better.

While I added ME into it, I also added an apologetic tone to it. 'This is my way but I know it's probably not yours' and 'I don't want you to think I'm telling you what to do' and so on. I was essentially writing as if I wasn't quite sure of what I was writing.

It was certainly not powerful or inspiring.

Then I understood.

I needed to not pretend to be some pontificating professor with pie in his patootie, and I needed to claim what I was writing as my truth.

I needed to be me...vulnerably, honestly, unabashedly me.

## *There's nothing less inspiring than a book where the author is pretending to be something they aren't.*

A client sent me the start to her book. Now this woman is joyous and magnetic and funny as shit. And I opened up this book and for some reason she sounded like a British versioned Mr. Roboto. It was dry and analytical and devoid of personality. So when I asked her what happened to her voice she simply answered "well I thought this is how I need to sound as an author." I said "sure, if you're writing a book on Ancient Geometric Physics" (which may or may not actually be a thing). But I reminded her that she's writing HER book and to use HER voice to do it, not some stick up the butt professor with little to no people skills.

To find your voice, speak in your voice. This goes back a bit to writing drunk...write without the pretense that you need to sound like an author to make an incredibly awesome book. You are an author simply in the act of writing a book, so it better be a book that represents who you are, not what you think you need to be.

You are enough.

### *Your voice is the perfect voice to tell your story and teach what you know.*

Use it. Whether it's airy-fairy-goddessy or sailor-on-leave-y, your voice is the only one you need for YOUR book.

# FRAUD *Alert*

You know when you're being a fraud? It's when you're pretending to be something you're not.

Stop it.

But if you're writing what you know and you're using your own authentic voice and you're not acting like some spiritual guru when you don't even like to meditate, then you can't possibly be a fraud can you?

*Writing a book makes us think we need to be something else, that suddenly our consciousness needs to be elevated to the nth power; when in fact we don't, we just need to be who we are right now.*

Everybody feels like a fraud at some point in this process. It's normal.

So if you're feeling that fraud vibe tickling the back of your brain, then ask yourself - am I being true to who I am in my writing right now?

Then adjust and keep writing.

Stay true to who you are and no one will ever accuse
you of being a fraud. Not even you…

# STORY *Time*

Your stories are valuable. There are three kinds of personal stories: stories about you, stories about your clients and stories about your mentors. Think of them as salt and pepper.

I don't care what kind of non-fiction book you're writing.

Don't write them without adding salt and pepper.

And if your book is an autobiography, add some stories about others in your life, your mentors, your peers.

Proper use of all the types of personal stories helps the reader know you, feel you, and see themselves in your book.

There's a reason all great religions use parable to teach...because stories are relatable. Pure fact is not as memorable as fact seasoned with story.

*Be a storyteller and season your book liberally.*

# WRITER'S Block

Hey gang, writer's block feels real and it's totally totally not. If suddenly you get stuck on a spot in your book it means that it's either a section you're not in alignment with, not interested in or you're missing something.

## *You can do a few of different things to get past this.*

1. Work on it for 3 minutes and see what comes up. Sometimes it's just a matter of not buying into the easy excuse of 'writer's block'.

2. You have a map…skip ahead to the next section, or to a section that sounds more fun or easier, and come back to this section. We think because a book is typically read from front to back that we need to write it that way. It's simply not true - you're a

creative person so create out of order in whatever manner you see fit.

3. Journal about why you're stuck on this particular section…yes, you heard that – write about why you're stuck. Why? Because sometimes it's because intuitively you know there's something off. I was writing a story once and I just couldn't get it out right. I deleted the first couple of paragraphs over and over again until it dawned on me – I was writing the story I 'should' write instead of the one I was scared to write – the one that would have so much more impact. The 'should' story got scrapped and the writer's block ended so I could move on.

4. Do anything BUT write for a while and come back later. Go wash your socks or eat a cupcake or sit in the sun or read a trashy novel or watch a Star Trek episode. Whatever you need to pattern disrupt your brain, do that. And then honor your book by giving it some love.

*If you still are feeling stuck, don't beat yourself up for it. Try again tomorrow.*

# SHOW YOUR *Work*

This is the MOST important chapter in this whole book. Seriously. I should actually cut and paste it multiple times so you don't miss it.

The number one mistake that most authors make is that they hoard their work until it's done and perfect.

## *Do Not Write In A Sterile Room*

## *Do Not Write In Isolation*

Share your work. Share what you're writing. Share that you're writing. Share the title. Share the struggles. Share the successes.

Show your work.

Show unedited sections as you write; you know, the drunken passages that still need smoothing out. Show the gold that you sift. Show a passage you're struggling with and get input.

Show your work.

Show it on Facebook. Email it to your list. Text it to your best friend. Make fliers and pass it out on the street. Whatever works for you.

## Why? For so many reasons...

First is that it keeps you accountable. If you show people you're writing and show them your progress, there's no going back. It's a commitment to a cause.

Second, it gets you used to showing your work. It makes it easier and easier to imagine sharing the whole book in the world.

Third, you'll get feedback – mostly people cheering you on, but also some honest comments that may help you work something else into the book that feels right.

Fourth is that showing your work helps you build up a reading base before you even publish. Sharing the whole process engages people at a different level, allowing them to take some ownership in the project, and they feel pride and excitement when the book finally comes out.

So get over the idea of writing in a bubble. The more you share and show, the better it is for your whole book writing process.

Show your damn book.

# DON'T BE *Grey*

It doesn't matter what you're writing, being vague and general helps no one.

Claim you.

Claim your message.

Own it.

Don't be foggy or unsure.

Don't hide behind large words without substance.

Don't make sweeping generalizations without backing them up.

## *There is no grey area in a book.*

Which is why so few people actually write their book. Because it can be frightening to be clear, or to state something they believe to be true so plainly. Vacillating doesn't belong in a book.

This is an internal job, to trust that you're being as clear as possible and then backing it up with stories and examples and tales.

*This is about you really leaning into being powerful and magnetic and super crystal clear.*

You've got this.

Step out of the grey.

## SECTION 03:
# FINISHING

# FINISHING, A.K.A.
## *Publishing...*

Because if you've gone through the steps of writing, if you've done your 3 minutes or your 30 minutes or your big ass sprint, this is where all the detail work comes into play.

And if there's something a creative mind likes less than consistency, it's details.

I'm not going to sit here and tell you that this is the encyclopedia to self-publishing, but these are the things you can't google, the things that my clients learn first; and then we go through the detailed checklists until that publish button is pushed. These are the people you want on your team - because self-publishing doesn't mean doing it all by yourself. These are the steps that make all other steps just a fancy dance.

These are the steps that make it easy for you to finish.

And that's what this is truly about right? Finishing…

# CREATE A *Team*

It is 100% possible to do this on your own. I've done it.

I've also done this with a team of amazing professionals.

I've lived both sides of the spectrum and I come to you begging you not to do this alone. Ever. Because there's nothing more soul sucking to a creative person than detail work. And if there's detail work to be done, it usually doesn't get done.

You're a writer so you need to focus on the writing. Finish that part and enroll others to help you with the rest. If you're going the traditional publishing route, then you need to get an agent, a publisher, work with a designer and an editor and a proofreader. If you're self-publishing, then bring in a creative editor, a designer and a proofreader.

These are non-negotiables in producing a quality piece of work.

Many people try to cut corners when self-publishing a book. I'm not telling you to hire Cadillac versions, but please take my experiences and learn from them - there is nothing more horrible than deleting that one extra space and wrecking the entire layout (that you'll need to fix 98 more times) because you didn't bother hiring a designer, or finding those typos in the printed copy of your book, the one you read 10 times trying to proofread yourself.

Get yourself a team of professionals who will make you look awesome.

Do not go it alone.

# GOING THE *Publisher* ROUTE

We are in an amazing time where we can literally upload our finished books and print out a copy immediately, upload it to Amazon and start selling it within a couple of days. Gone are the days where only the elite few were actually able to see their book in print.

There are pros and cons to both kinds of publishing, and even within the world of self-publishing there are different paths.

*I've learned from and worked with people on all sides of the equations and it boils down to this...*

If you're choosing the traditional route of getting an agent and publisher, they will set you up with their team and some perks in return for future profits for them. The payout per book depends on the contract you negotiate. You will need to find the right agent who is willing to take you on, who believes in your ability to sell this book.

Notice I said sell the book not write the book. Quality content is not hard to come by. An amazing project is not that difficult to find. What do publishers want? Someone who can take that amazing project and sell the crap out of it and get as many copies into the world as possible. They want a personality they can stand behind and create a movement of future profitable projects moving forward.

If this is the route you really desire, then stop writing and start building your brand. Build a following. Put the pieces into place to have a great platform to take off from. Your job is to write a killer proposal and create a platform that will make a publisher think that this book will succeed.

*Because most publishers rely on you to do the bulk of the marketing. So before you send in that proposal, you need to start marketing.*

That said, the mistake that many writers who want to go the traditional publisher route make is that they send in the proposal, or proposals, and they wait. They wait for the news that their project has been accepted.

If this is your path - DON'T JUST WAIT. Send those proposals…build your platform and keep writing.

Because here's a little secret back door tip for you. If you really want to be published with a publisher, have a successful book first. One of my friends just got a dream publishing deal; the kind where they pay her lots of money, send her on book tours and help promote her - not because she had a great proposal, but because her previous self-published book was wildly popular. Because she not only built her platform, she proved that she had the brand required to really elevate that product.

I have another friend who has a highly successful book and he's had plenty of publishers approach him with deals. And he refused them, because he's making more money self-publishing. That said, he did sign on with a publisher who is bringing the book into 11 countries and translating it into other languages, something he wasn't going to do for himself.

One more? How about the friend who got the deal with the dream publisher and then completely burned out because she couldn't keep up with the marketing and PR demands of the publisher.

Which brings us right back to self-publishing doesn't it? Or at least sending out for publishing deals while you continue on the self-publishing path.

Because there are only 2 kinds of authors in the world - published ones and unpublished ones. You can wait to be picked up - and some of you will be - or you can plant the seeds and continue writing the damn book.

# SELF-Publishing

Even in the realm of self-publishing you've got options. There is a pay-to-play option, where you pay someone to be your publisher. I guess that's sort of a hybrid at the end of the day, except that the publisher is simply a paid partner that navigates some of the techy things for you. And I'm all for pay-to-play if you consider the fact that you really need a team to do something, and a publisher is a valid team member for you.

There are many different individuals and companies that offer these services and they all have their pros and cons.

To truly self-publish means to do the whole enchilada. It doesn't mean you're doing it alone, but it means that you are the boss, this is your project and you are in charge of seeing it through.

That intimidates some people and seems overwhelming. It's the reason why people don't write their books while waiting and hoping for a conventional publisher to pick them up.

I had a gal message me the other day to ask me if I could give her any tips on getting her 2 books published. I asked if she'd considered self-publishing. Her reply? "I would honestly feel like a failure if I did that".

I get it. There is prestige in having a publisher.

There's also the fact that she's sitting on 2 books that aren't any closer to being out in the world.

*For me? Failure is waiting for someone else to determine my fate. For me, publishing my books is more important than signing a contract.*

I personally love being self-published. All the rights are mine, I can edit it, delete it, make an audio copy of it, give it away, translate it into pig Latin. For me, self-publishing isn't about what someone else can do for me, it's about what I can make come true for myself.

(Side note so we're clear - it doesn't matter how it gets published, you are still responsible for writing and marketing the book. This publishing piece is actually peanut sized compared to those tasks but it stops people time and time again.)

*Your publishing success is only as strong as the team you build around you and the effort you put into the experiment to begin with.*

All of my clients are self-published. They work with me and I gather their team for them. At the end of the day however, they get to have full control of their book and the back end of their book, so they can make changes anytime they want. I have friends who have paid others significant money to publish their books for them and to use their teams and such, but they don't get reports on how their book is performing and they have to jump through hoops to make any changes to the book itself, even if they find a typo. That's just not sexy to me when gathering your own team just isn't that hard to do.

I will say here that I prefer a print on demand method with the capability to give multiple book discounts. Each company offers different pricing and delivery methods but I would choose one that has the ability to distribute automatically to at least Amazon. For an electronic book, like Kindle, there are a few places you can publish, including Kindle, Barnes & Noble and the iTunes Store.

Because digital books are so simple to publish, many choose to do that first, with no hard copy book at all. I prefer to have both available, but they need to be treated differently – the layout demands are different for print and digital books. I chose to publish 'Unconventional Wisdom' both ways but 'Your Inner Council' is ONLY available as a print book because the layout and design don't translate to an electronic reading device. I got a little fancy with it.

## You don't have to choose how you're publishing before you start writing.

Write!

Finish the book and then assess what the most important thing for you is… getting support from a publisher or getting your book out into the world.

# WHY WORD

Typing on the computer doesn't suck, and Word itself does not suck. I've used it. I've used GoogleDocs and I've used Scrivener (which is my favorite). However once in a while you've gotta take the writing offline.

Because you can't see the flow of the book in an electronic document.

You can read and write on the screen all day long but as you get closer to finishing that book do yourself a favor...print the whole thing out.

## *Nothing beats old school paper when it comes to finishing your book.*

Because before you go to editing and proofing, you need to take a moment and feel and see what you've created.

Word is great for everything but giving you the feeling that you've just written a book.

And no feeling beats that.

Write all you want on Word but do yourself a favor and print it out from time to time just to see what you've been up to. Something about having physical evidence does wonders for your creativity.

And before you publish anything, read that hard copy and edit from there.

# *Editing*

A real editor helps you refine your vision, makes sure your voice is shining through, points out where you need more explaining or more stories, or where you need less. They don't get concerned with typos or spelling mistakes, although they may catch some anyway. They are the big vision holders who keep you on your path.

And I'll be honest, not every book needs this level of editing.

If you want someone from day one to carry you through to publishing, hire a book coach / creative editor. This editor will help you refine your message and why you want to write. This person will help you tap into what that reader gets out of the book and hold you to that. They will also help you redefine what you think you 'should' be writing, or what a book 'should' look like and what you want it to be.

Writing 'Your Inner Council' was scary for me. It was the first book I'd written by myself and hiring that Creative & Developmental Editor/Coach was incredible helpful. After that first draft she asked me 'Where are your stories? You're a storyteller, you need to write stories." And then we dumped out all my stories and started sifting through them together. It was like having a partner to help me through the creative hiccups. It's what I do for my clients, taking them through the fears and resistance and keeping them on task.

If you want someone to take what you've written and make comments on it, an editor is fabulous to have. Don't publish a book without someone reading through it for consistency, to find holes in the story or the information, to point out where you're rambling or for a second pair of eyes to make sure you're making sense.

I'll also add, just knowing I've hired someone to help me develop my books helps me stay on task. My creative editor gave me pep talks and I felt like the project and I were being held.

Yes, it's totally okay to hire a friend to do this.

No, I personally hire professionals.

*Because someone who does this professionally will always be able to guide you better. They won't hold back when something doesn't make sense. They won't mix up their personal knowledge of you and what you're saying with what's actually on the page.*

That said, I wouldn't just hire anyone. I would only hire someone who was interested in what I was writing, who can see the vision of the change I'm hoping to create and is able to buy into it. I will only hire someone who is going to step up to be a partner of sorts and will feel responsible for the results, and who believes in the project. This is critically important to me; and those people who go through my 'Writing The Damn Book' Retreats and Programs benefit from my experiences of what true creative support feels like.

It keeps you focused and on target for the beautiful piece of art you most dream of creating, and it's worth so much to be able to know at the end of the day that your book is the best it could be.

# Proofreading

No matter what you do, do NOT proofread your own book. Hire someone. Period.

*Because you're too close to your own book to really see the little things. Because spellcheck doesn't make sure you're using the its and it's correctly. Because there is nothing more insulting to a reader than you showing you don't care enough about them to proofread the damn book.*

I read a few books every week, and when I go to give that book stars on Goodreads and Amazon, they automatically get one less star if there are typos.

It doesn't have to cost much, around $200 - $300 depending on the length of your book. But it's an investment that you need to make.

A good proofreader or copy editor should comb through your work several times, and yes, they will make corrections every time.

A super easy way to do this? Upload your book to Google Docs and share the file with them. They can go into edit suggesting mode and mark up the book electronically, they can ask you questions and make suggestions (like 'do you mean this…?' Or 'this sentence isn't making sense'). Then you can go through and accept the changes and answer questions. Go 3-4 rounds like this and your book is ready to roll.

# Design

The best authors are not the ones writing in a vacuum. They're the ones who get support.

Here's the thing, interior layout is kind of a pain in the butt. Making sure the page margins look good and the headers are consistent and that one extra space doesn't shuffle the pages for all the chapter beginnings. And print books and electronic books have different layout requirements so you need to do it all twice.

But it's possible and if you're really wanting to shave costs, learn all you can about laying out a book. Createspace has great tutorials and guidelines and templates for you to follow.

## What you should not do is create the cover on your own.

Hire someone for at least the front and back covers.

## Because 'never judge a book by its cover' in the world of real books is a lie. What happens there impacts how people respond to your book.

That said, don't just hire a designer and tell them to have at it. Have an idea of what you're looking for. Create a Pinterest board of other books you really like the covers of. Go to the bookstore and snap photos of books that inspire you – not because of the content but because of how they look. The more information about your book, what's inside the book, and what feeling you'd like in the design, the easier it is for a good designer to give you what you're asking for.

Hey, and while you're at the bookstore, also be a total geek and take a measuring tape…because knowing what size you want your book to be is also pretty damn important. It's part of the design process.

So look for style and look for size and start collecting a vision board of sorts to be able to hand over and say – this is where I want to go.

## Ask for referrals. Interview a couple of designers. Get a couple of quotes. Look at the work they've done.

Note – do NOT send them a copy of the book before you've gotten to your final draft. Once it's been laid out, you want to be able to do one quick run through and hit publish. Most designers will only give you up to 3 change reviews, so be certain that you've got your final text ready to roll before you send it to them. Multiple design changes because there's a bunch of typos or rewrites does no one any favors. Hire the designer and then have them wait until it's almost ready to roll out to the public.

# Re-Read

You know the saying about not seeing the forest through the trees?

You've been working IN your book for a while. You know each sentence and all the words and you've been knee deep in trees.

There's this point when everyone's done their editing and the design work. There are no changes to be made.

Grab yourself a cuppa and sink in for some quality enjoying.

## *Most authors miss this part.*

They feel like they've read it a million times before publication.

They haven't.

They've been looking at the trees.

*There is nothing quite as eye-opening and engaging as sitting down and truly taking the time to realize what you just did. That you have finished writing a freaking book!*

Read it.

Enjoy it.

Bask in your brilliance.

Celebrate your awesomeness.

Make notes of what you'll change for the NEXT revision…don't let them stop you from publishing now.

This is not a time to work, it's a time to appreciate and enjoy.

Because you just did what thousands of people around the world are still dreaming of.

And I'm sending you hugs for it!

# WHAT'S IN A *Name?*

The name of your book absolutely does matter. It should be relevant and catchy and represent what you're writing…it should take that end result and sum it up.

*Allow the title of your book to change as you write it. Refine it as you go.*

But the title of your book is nowhere near as important as the tag line underneath it.

Why?

Here's a little mind bend for you - Amazon is nothing more than a great big search engine, driven by keywords and relevancy.

If you don't touch on the key ideas in the book

in the tag line, you're missing out on wonderful traffic and attention. AND if the reader has a hard time figuring out what you're writing about, they probably won't buy the book.

Don't count on the description to sell it…most people will eye-drift through the titles and choose the one that is most on target for what they want to learn about. Yes, the design counts, but that tag line is key.

It's the #1 thing I screwed up on with my first book 'Unconventional Wisdom: Stories Beyond The Mind To Awaken The Heart." Kind of makes you go 'huh' right? And while we were fortunate enough for the book to gain Bestseller status, it is a more confusing book for people to want to purchase because they don't know what it is about right away.

## *Make it easy for people to find you and to know that your book is what they want.*

What are those end results you want to create? What are the key ideas of the book? What do you desire most to help people change?

Then do the online research - search on Amazon for some of your keywords - what books also come up when you search for them? Are they relevant? If they are then you're on to something. If sprinkler parts show up instead of books, then perhaps people looking for books aren't searching for that word (unless your book is actually on sprinkler parts of course). You want to see books that are using those words – maybe not thousands of books, but some books for sure.

Keep a page in your book journal dedicated to little sentences and phrases that apply and then keep simmering them down. Ask your editor to help. Ask your Facebook friends to help you pick one or two.

Pay as much attention to the tag line as you can because what's in a name does count.

# THE BOOK
*Description*

Think of your book description as the ultimate landing page.

Our inner author wants to write a terribly clever book description, to wax poetic so to speak. But if there is one piece where a professional copywriter would earn their fee, it's here.

*The book description is not an extension of your writing. The description is ultimately about sales, and it's an important piece of the puzzle to get people to truly excited about reading your book.*

My description of 'Unconventional Wisdom' was seriously horrible. We were fortunate enough to drive enough traffic to the book to get Bestseller status but it wasn't quite right. I hired a guy who specializes in book descriptions to update the copy for Amazon and sales rose. It's still to this day not quite right and may take a couple more rounds to get it just so. And I recognize that book was a grand experiment in everything I could do wrong in publishing a book.

You don't need to hire a professional but it's important that you understand that the book description is where you get to really simmer down the whole book, what it solves, who your reader is going to be after they read this book. It's also a ready cool place for endorsements if you can get them.

This is your book in concentrated form, created for the sole purpose of making people want to read the book.

So take your time with this.

Write down everything you want to tell people about the book and then start editing it over and over again until it's succinct and draws people in. A really great way to start is by asking a question of your reader they will say yes to. For example, "Have you ever struggled with your weight?" And then go from there…

## *Be prepared to edit this short piece even more than your book.*

Use it in your description of the book on the back of the book (with a short bio of you) and everywhere you list the book for sale - Amazon etc.

# AUTHOR *Page*

I'll be honest - having an Author Page on Amazon might be one of the coolest things ever. Why? Because it feels official…'Look, I'm an Author'.

*I don't know why more authors don't create an author page, because it's super fun! Make sure you take the opportunity to create author pages everywhere.*

Obviously a bio is part of that page but I want to drop a little extra spice here…because this is also an opportunity to send people to your book site. Why? Because people who buy your book from a site aren't really in your inner circle. You want to be able to play with them more, draw them in and create a stronger community of support for your work and for them. Offer a free gift. Woo them. This is about you and it isn't. I'll explain more in the next section on sharing your work but this is part of the publishing cycle - to remember to not just post your book but to create a great profile.

# HIT  Publish

*There is nothing more exciting than hitting that publish button and feeling like 'holy shit, I did it'.*

And there's nothing more disappointing than sitting there for days waiting to actually see the results of the button push. Because it takes a few days for the book to show up anywhere...and it feels totally anticlimactic.

So plan ahead. If you want a launch date of May 10, don't hit publish on May 9 and expect it to be up and for sale on Amazon. Timing wise this was a bit of a surprise for me.

Plan on hitting that button a few days in advance - although a week is even better. Do it secretly. Make adjustments to how it looks online. Attach it to your Author Page. Make sure the description looks good, that the layout is right. Give yourself a buffer to address the unexpected. You may have a few friends sneak in early and buy a copy or leave a review but truly, plan ahead of your announcement that the book is live and give yourself that breathing room.

# SECTION 04:

# SHARING

# NOW What?

The book is done. You've hit publish.

Now there's the task of getting that book into the hands of readers right?

This part of your book creation starts the second you sit down to write your book.

It starts when you are showing your work as you write.

It starts when you design the cover and create the back cover copy.

*Honestly, it actually starts when you dream of writing a book that can change one person's life.*

Sharing your work with the world is the number two job of being an author, the first being the actual writing.

job of being an author, the first being the actual
Honestly, it actually starts when you dream

There are thousands of programs and books on how to create a bestselling book and strategies to have thousands of readers. There are some geniuses in the world of book marketing.

For ME, the most important part of having written a book is connecting with my readers, soul to soul. I love those emails I get from people telling me that they felt like they could see themselves in my book, that there was a connection between us instantly. And then they become a part of my circle and support me and my work in beautiful ways.

I love sharing my books as a way of building my community first and foremost, so this section will reflect that. I won't be talking to you about funnels or landing pages. There's an energetic component that sharing entails…let's play there.

*Because there's nothing more beautiful than seeing that first review on Amazon, tears in your eyes, knowing that you've made an impact and then having that person become a part of your extended book family.*

This section is for you to lean into open-hearted and genuine sharing of your work. This is about celebrating your awesomeness for having written the damn book.

# YOUR

Responsibility

Creatives aren't always the best marketers.

But the best marketers are always the most creative… because they have a vision for something, and they create that in the world. They envision their widget to be the bestselling widget in history, they believe their widget is the best around and they create a platform for that widget to appear even cooler, more needed, more desired than all other widgets.

Your book is that widget.

*No pressure here - because I can feel that moment of 'oh shit-ness'. To think of your book as the best widget ever feels like your head just grew like 50 times, right? Who are you to…?*

Well it's time to stop the false humility. This isn't about bragging. This isn't about creating false promises. And this isn't about selling tons and tons of books.

Remember in that first section where we dove into what your book has been created for? Remember that reader who was changed at the end of your book? That person doesn't even know they need to read your book right now... but they do.

This is about telling that person that your widget is ready and waiting for them. It was designed to be exactly what they need right now.

You get to be creative and lovingly say - hey, I created this widget specifically for you. It's my gift.

*What I'd love for you as a creative soul to truly understand is that it doesn't have to be a brain project to create the perfect marketing scheme to get your book 'out there'. This is a time to use that creativity and that vulnerability and make something magical and personal to you.*

This book is your gift to the world.

And you dishonor that gift when you hold it back from being read.

It is your responsibility to take this Source-given gift and make sure it gets seen.

You don't need to employ a marketing strategy that doesn't feel right for you. You simply must remember that you have done something miraculous and sharing it helps you grow too.

*Because the miracle isn't over when you're done writing. The miracle happens when someone is done reading.*

How creative can you get? How can you gift wrap this book up and give it to the world?

Make the shift from seeing marketing as something outside of your desired skill set, and understand that it's simply an extension of sharing your message, that it's part of the authoring process.

# BESTSELLER, BESTSELLING OR BEST *Impacting*

My first book, "Unconventional Wisdom" was a Bestseller. It topped the charts on Amazon in a few different categories. And it's really really cool to be able to say that I am a Bestselling Author.

AND that doesn't mean I made tons of money on the book or that it reached thousands of people. (Actually as a side note, I donate all the proceeds from that book to micro loans on Kiva). It meant that I did specific things for the keywords and the placement of category for my book that allowed it to reach #1 status during a few days where we gave away the book. Essentially Amazon is a giant search engine that responds well to SEO strategies.

And if your eyes just glazed over, stay with me.

"Your Inner Council" was a totally different story. To date, it has sold more copies than "Unconventional Wisdom" but has never been a Bestseller. I didn't publish a Kindle copy where bestsellers are made more easily, only a print copy.

It wasn't even the 'smart' book to publish. It wasn't about my business. It wasn't laced with ads to hire me as a coach or take my courses. It was subtly seeded but that was all. It wasn't the calling card that I could have written. It was a spiritual journey and a way of working with our intuition by starting a dialog with the highest voices within ourselves. It was the book I wanted to write, was guided to write.

*And within a couple of weeks of it being published, my business filled up with clients who couldn't wait to work with me, who had read the book, or seen my unique way of releasing it into the world, and wanted to be a part of my circle.*

I didn't set out to write a Bestseller.

And I didn't market the hell out of it to create a Bestselling book.

I wanted it to make a real impact on people's lives and give them a new way to make intuition a priority.

## I wanted a Best Impacting book.

It does make money for me every day. It could very well be a Bestseller someday. But the bottom line is that it makes a difference for people and that was my highest and greatest dream for it.

So decide where you want to go with your book now, because each has a different slant.

To create a Bestseller, start brushing up on your SEO tactics, do research on the thousands of programs to help you create that.

Perhaps it's more interesting to create a Bestselling book, one that sells millions of copies worldwide. That requires some serious marketing and PR, it requires you to do the book tours and talk on podcasts and on stages. That's a sexy path for a lot of authors and there are thousands of programs to help you create that too.

## But to make a difference with your book? That's the sexy work for me.

And that starts on Day 1 and continues every single day.

Yes, of course, a well written concept and book help, but it means nothing if no one ever reads it right?

Now let's get it into hands.

# GIVE *First*

This is always my mantra in business. Give First. It starts with showing your work as you go. I give full sections of my book out as posts and emails. I give my inspiration out because what I write is good stuff.

## And when it came to the book, I started giving it away as it was complete.

I gave my list access to the first 3 sections (about 50 pages).

And then, I gave them another 3 sections when those were done.

And then, I gave them the full pdf version of the print book when the book was published.

And then, I gave a workbook to go with the book.

And then, I have a quick start method for those who wanted an easier way to work with their Inner Council.

And I continue to gift people with hard copies and electronic copies all of the time.

Why?

Because 'Give First'.

Forget the strategy – love on your people.

Give them a free book. Send them two so they can give one to a friend. Offer them bulk discounts. Give them bonuses. Create a free Q&A call.

## Don't hold back on your generosity or love.

Because this is your GIFT to the world.

# YOUR BOOK

Imagine that you have a group of dedicated people who cannot wait to read the book, share the book, talk about the book, leave reviews for the book… before you've even hit that publish button.

*This is your inner circle of awesomeness… these are the people you get to treat like the amazing benevolent beings they truly are.*

These are your Book Angels.

And you get to create them…

I gave first to my Angels.

I made an offer to my list and to my Facebook peeps. I let them know that the first few chapters were ready to view. I asked the people who wanted to read those early chapters to become my Book Angels.

As an Angel they got those first few chapters and then the next few and then before the book launched they would get the whole book. I also gifted them with a call a month after the book was released.

And in return I asked that they be on my team. That they leave reviews and that they share my posts and that they tell their friends about my book.

On the day of my launch, my book went viral on Facebook.

And I only posted about it ONCE.

## My book angels were instrumental to the success of that book.

And will be forever on my team as I add more and more to the crew.

Releasing a book is vulnerable. It feels edgy. Will they like it? Will I get horrible reviews? Will anyone buy it?

Having Angels in place gave me a sense of warmth and security and community so that I wasn't nervous about hitting that publish button.

Set yourself up to succeed by not expecting to do it alone. Most of my sales in those first few weeks branched out from my Angels posting up pages from the book, talking about how great it was, being ambassadors for what I do. And bonus? They also caught a single annoying typo before the book hit print.

# LOVE THEM Up

Okay - this is worth saying over and over again… don't market to people. Love them up. I remember talking to my team prior to our launches. On the surface we had a pretty traditional funnel, getting people to move from one place to the next, getting them on the list and then adding them to my community.

But we had a very different intention.

It was never about selling more books or getting those emails.

## It was ALWAYS how can we love on my readers more?

How can I inspire them more?

How can I give more?

How can I support them more?

Our motto was - it doesn't matter if we sell one copy. It matters that everyone feels a part of a movement, that everyone feels the love. Because publishing books is a journey of love, let's bring that into everything we do.

Funnel or no funnel. Sales or no sales.

Nothing happens without us leading with our heart.

And it showed.

A week after that second book launched I was hired by a client who said "I want you to be my coach because I watched that launch and I've never experienced anything like it. It was so loving and supportive and warm and I want to bring more of that approach into my business."

## *Lead with love and give even more.*

Not only will your people feel it and love it, it will make all the difference in the world to your stress levels as you release your book using 'love' energy to drive you rather than 'sell' energy.

# BUILDING YOUR *Tribe*

I can't say 'love them up' without adding that you also get to 'build them up'. Your book is an amazing tool to build and grow your own community. I could call this list building, which at its core, it is. But let's dial that up a bit.

Because a list isn't anything special.

## Connection and community - those are everything.

How much can you love on these people?

This is the give, give, give philosophy all over again.

Give them value. Give them gifts. Give them pieces of your creation.

Ask only for them to join your group or your email tribe.

## Why? So you can love on them some more.

See here's the real fact about selling a book.

It's a one way transaction.

It's not the start of a dialogue.

That's up to you to create.

It's up to you to say "hey, here's my stuff. Can I send you more?" That's how you create a two-way dialogue. That's how you create that connection.

I was sitting with a friend of mine, who also happens to be an amazing publisher, discussing scalability and how books can help you scale your business differently and I said 'You know, I don't care how many books I sell as long as I know that one person is impacted and that one person and I connect'. And he nodded and said simply, 'then we just need to find ways for you to feel connected with one person thousands of times over'. And that's it right there…because in order for me to love on someone, I can't just put a book online and have them buy it. I want to be with them on a journey.

Building your tribe is about so much more than how many names you get on your email list.

It's about how many people you can connect with, and make a long term impact on.

# Reviews

Your Book Angels and your Tribe are important for more reasons than just helping you spread the word about your book. Here's a little ninja secret about Amazon and other booksellers - relevancy is critical.

See if we understand that Amazon is nothing more than a search engine and we set up our keywords (search terms so people can find your book), that's half the battle. Amazon also wants to know that when people do search for your topic and buy your book that it's what they actually wanted. Those stars and reviews tell Amazon where to place you when buyers are looking for a book to purchase.

Those reviews are also really important for people who happen across your book and are deciding whether to buy it. Social proof that it's something worth reading is one of the most impactful strategies you can employ when promoting your work.

And you don't have to do anything for it.

*Well, almost.*

Most people won't leave a review - they don't want to be visible, they don't know what to say, they don't think to do it, or it's a non-critical task on their to-do list, etc.

That's another reason to love up on your Book Angels, because they will be your first line of offense - they are the ones you can ask for honest reviews online. In fact I set it up in our agreement as an Angel. I give and give to them and ask in return that they help me share the book on the day we release it and to leave a review that day as well.

For the people who join my list from the ads inside the book? I ask them for reviews as well.

*Your job is to help remind your people to give reviews and to set yourself up to get those beautiful stars.*

I'll add that the emotional benefit of reading good reviews is amazing and continually brings tears to my eyes. And the bad reviews? Well, those happen sometimes too. So it helps to know that your Angels are there loving up on you. Print out the positive ones, put them all over your wall and move on.

# DON'T JUST GIVE *One Book*

There are people you'll want to send copies of your book to. Do it. Don't hesitate. Get this book into people's hands.

This is a part of loving them up.

It will cost you money to print the book and ship it or hand it to them.

Spend it.

But don't stop there.

Send them not one, but two copies.

*Because you're so excited to give them a copy that you know they would love to share too.*

Here's a copy for you and for a friend you know will enjoy it too.

Because there's nothing better than paying it forward. Because there's nothing better than creating your own viral movement. Because there's nothing better than getting introduced to someone through a friend rather than showing up as a stranger at their door.

Give two because it feels good, and because it's an endorsement that will keep giving.

# FREE—*dom*

There are a lot of strategies around giving the kindle version of your book away for free. There are pros and cons. Now, I normally have no problem giving away my books but I had a hard time giving away 'Unconditional Wisdom' online, because I set that book up so that the profits went directly into a loan with Kiva as a charitable donation.

And if I gave it away, then how would I give a new loan to someone in need?

*So instead of waiting for the profits, I just understood that I would personally fund a loan for every 100 downloads.*

Mischief managed and loans made.

And it was during the time it was free that the book reached Bestseller status.

There is never a reason not to gift your work to the world, that's the purpose of creating it.

So if you're uncomfortable with giving away your art, ask why. For me it wasn't because I didn't want to love on my people, but because I wanted to meet my commitment to micro lending. Once I understood that, I was very happy to share the book for free and commit to supporting the loans anyway.

There is sound marketing evidence to back up giving your book away for free on Kindle. It's how most books reach bestseller status and it helps drive up reviews as well. Your primary job at this stage is to get the book into people's hands. This is a fun, generous, pay-it-forward way to do that.

Use the free days to drum up downloads, or use them to give to your angels (and only let them know it's free for a day). It doesn't matter why, it's the energy of give and then give more. Love up on your people by sharing without hesitation.

# SEND THE *PDF*

If Kindle isn't your thing, that's okay. Send the full pdf version of your book to read. There are countries where my book is not available or where it's price prohibitive to order so when people email me and ask if there's an electronic version, I send then the pdf free of charge.

I also gave my Book Angels free pdf versions before the print copy came out.

I send it off to people who are curious about my work.

I gave it as a bonus for purchasing my hard copy online (as a great way of building my community list).

*Your book is an amazing gift to the world. Be creative with how you wrap it up and then give it with wild abandon.*

# BULK IT Up

This isn't something that's going to apply to everyone…but if you can see that your book will be useful to many at once instead of one at a time, then let's go bulk.

*Because there's a beauty to self-publishing a print-on-demand book: you can set any price and sell any amount of copies.*

So for some of you a really fun and sexy thing to do is to sell copies in bulk.

Your people can buy 3, 5, 10, 15, 25, 50 - even 100 books at a time from you for discounts. This is also great for speakers who are negotiating speaking contracts. You can even opt to waive the fee and ask the producer to purchase books for the audience instead. Get creative and get that book into their hands.

Not only can your readers get discounted pricing on multiple copies (because you can order it directly from the printer and bypass Amazon restrictions), but you have a really great opportunity to offer more love and gifts the more people buy. For this to really work, you'll need a dedicated page and some pretty juicy gifts. This is a magical way of loving on your people on steroids.

It's also a beautiful way of opening up your readers to understand the paying it forward type of generosity, to get them to think about who would benefit from this information and then get it into their hands.

# THE INSIDE *Ad*

I'll say it straight here - you have no idea who is buying your book on Amazon. None. No names or emails. No indication that it's even been purchased unless you go into the backend site.

So how can you encourage people to be a part of your community?

Well they've got your book in their hands…

*How about an ad inside the book? One in the front couple of pages and one at the end.*

This isn't smarmy or presumptuous if it's an offer for something related and of value. For Your Inner Council, there's an ad to a free companion workbook that goes along with working with your own intuition and starting those dialogues with your inner council. It's 12 pages and it's pretty awesome. I have clients who use that workbook all of the time.

And I get downloads from that little ad from a decent percent of my readers…which is super fun, like a walking timeline of purchases. And I know these people won't just read the book, they will read it and do something with the information; they are into the book for true experiential transformation rather than for another book on their shelf. And those are my people, the ones who will take action towards their dreams and who are actively expanding who they are in the world.

*It's the perfect filter for my business and for the people I naturally want to love on even more.*

So an ad inside of your book is nothing more than an invitation to make this a two-way conversation. You can build your community in more ways than one, but adding that little seed in the front and back makes it easy for people to actually connect with you.

# THE

I will confess that I have a URL addiction. I instantly buy the URL for my book before I start writing it, or as new names come to me. In fact I won't name the book until I've checked to see if the URL is available.

That said, it is not necessary that you have a dedicated website for your book. But if you'd truly like to build your book community, at least create a webpage where people can go and sign up for more gifts. This can be as simple as getting a free account on MailChimp and setting up a sign up page with them that includes a picture of your book so people know it's you. It can be as complex as creating an entire site dedicated to the highest and best outcome of this creation of yours. Or it can be a part of your existing business site.

It doesn't matter, no matter what you've been told.

*The only requirement here is that you look at this not as a place of advertisement but as a place to give those gifts and love on your community moving forward.*

# PR NOT
*Marketing*

In the world of book longevity, marketing sucks.

It's GREAT for short term gain…but if you want long term awesomeness and aren't concerned with making #1 (which doesn't truly help your book), then learn all you can from PR giants, not marketing gurus.

PR is loving and gentle, it requires us to talk and write to people. It's not about hitting people over the head with a Facebook ad, but wooing them.

I have a friend who makes hundreds of thousands of dollars from book sales each year. His strategy involved little marketing. Instead he focused on getting interviewed on people's podcasts. He has done well over 200 interviews and is an extreme hustler…I'm not suggesting this is THE way. But I am suggesting that instead of going out trying to build your own readership, you allow others to do the work for you. Writing articles for blogs, doing interviews and public speaking gigs are an amazing way of getting your book into the world without having to market.

Now before you argue that it's the same thing - it isn't. And there's nothing wrong with marketing, but so many people get STUCK around marketing that it's silly not to consider other pathways. The marketing is not the hard part of publishing a book if you lean into ways that fit who you are, and for most authors, writing and talking about your work is a natural path.

# SHARE PAST Go

This piece is as important here as it is when you're just starting the book. Whatever you write, you must be in love with it. You must love the message and be passionate about sharing it with others.

*Because sharing the book doesn't end after you release it into the world.*

Sharing the book over and over and over again is the magic. It's the difference between books that languish and books that thrive. When we honor our creation and continuously share it in the world a few things happen.

More people will read it and be impacted by it.

More love will circulate.

And it will feel good to create more creations. When we go through all the effort and turmoil to write a book, it's damn rude to set it aside and be done with it. When we are rude about creating things, our mind will be less inclined to write another book.

When we honor it however, our minds get on board because there is longevity there. We can feel the heart of the work beating. We know that it's safe to create. And we know it feels fricking amazing.

To start with an idea, a nudge, a dream.

To write the whole book, from map to final edit.

To publish your book and see it in your hands for the first time, fresh unsullied pages dripping with potentiality.

And to share it with the world over and over again, to impact each person who touches it in some way, and to connect with others who need and want what you've created from scratch.

## *This is the journey to being an author.*

To be writing the damn book one day and then to be on the other side, realizing a dream that few will ever see, will ever feel and will ever know.

# THE Beginning

It's funny to me that ending this book was hard for me, because I know that the end of this book indicates the beginning of yours. It's an opening, a way of chunking this huge ass project down into 4 basic sections.

I'm surrounded every day by people who had a deep desire to write a book, who are filled with fear and overwhelm. These same people feel like they have plenty of time to get to it.

I tell my clients all the time that if they really want to experience deep levels of self-growth, write a book. It brings up self-doubt, anxiety, disappointment, vulnerability, visibility, and it brings to you hope, big ass visions, dreams, and clarity of purpose. And it helps you fine tune your message to the world. It is the ultimate course in self-development and self-trust.

## And if you're going to commit to the path, be willing to jump in with both feet.

Even when you don't feel like writing.

Even when you feel like you don't have time to write.

Even when you're not sure if anyone will like your book. Or if they will even read it.

Even when you think it's too much work.

## Write.

Inevitably, in the first call we have after my book writing retreats, my clients bring a whole string of reasons why the book hasn't been worked on much. Life happened and got in the way.

And that's when I get to remind my clients that writing is a way of life, and that we can all switch around our priorities just a wee bit to do the very thing we set out to do.

Which is of course, to write and finish and publish that damn book.

# READY TO
*Publish?*

Download your handy-dandy one page
Publishing Checklist at:

*wrtitingthedamnbook.com/checklist*

so you can not just Write the Damn
book, but Finish It as well!!!

Printed in Great Britain
by Amazon